HOMESTEAD YOUR HOUSE

By California Attorneys Ralph Warner
Charles E. Sherman & Toni Lynne Ihara

Sixth Edition Revisions: Stephen Elias &
Mary Randolph

NOLO PRESS ▽ 950 Parker Street, Berkeley, CA 94710

PRINTING HISTORY

Nolo Press is committed to keeping its books up-to-date. Each new printing, whether or not it is called a new edition, has been completely revised to reflect the latest law changes. This book was printed and updated on the last date indicated below. Before you rely on information in it, you might wish to call Nolo Press (415) 549-1976 to check whether a later printing or edition has been issued.

Difference between new *editions* and *printings:*

New printing means there have been some minor changes, but usually not enough so that people will need to trade in or discard an earlier printing of the same edition. Obviously, this is a judgment call and any change, no matter how minor, might affect you.

New edition means one or more major - or a number of minor - law changes since the previous edition.

First Edition	1973
Second Edition	1975
Revised 2nd	1976
Third Edition	1978
Fourth Edition	1981
Fifth Edition	September 1983
2nd Printing	November 1984
Sixth Edition	January 1986
2nd Printing	September 1986

IMPORTANT

Although care has been taken to ensure the accuracy and utility of the information and forms contained in this book, neither Nolo Press nor the authors assume any liability in connection with any use of the information or forms contained herein.

ISBN 0-87337-011-2

UPDATE SERVICE

■ Introductory Offer ■

Our books are as current as we can make them, but sometimes the laws do change between editions. You can read about law changes which may affect this book in the NOLO NEWS, a 16-page newspaper which we publish quarterly.

In addition to the Update Service, each issue contains comprehensive articles, about the growing self-help law movement as well as areas of the law that are sure to affect you. **(regular subscription rate is $7.00)**

To receive the next 4 issues of the NOLO NEWS, please send us $2.00.

Name ____

Address ____

____

Send to: NOLO PRESS, 950 Parker St., Berkeley, CA 94710

HYH 9/86

Recycle Your Out-of-Date Books & Get One Third off your next purchase!

Using an old edition can be dangerous if information in it is wrong. Unfortunately, laws and legal procedure change often. To help you keep up to date we extend this offer. If you cut out and deliver to us the title portion of the cover of any old Nolo book we'll give you a 33% discount off the retail price of any new Nolo book. For example, if you have a copy of TENANTS' RIGHTS, 4th edition and want to trade it for the latest CALIFORNIA MARRIAGE AND DIVORCE LAW, send us the TENANTS' RIGHTS cover and a check for the current price of MARRIAGE & DIVORCE, less a 33% discount. Information on current prices and editions are listed in the Nolo News (see above box). Generally speaking, any book more than two years old is of questionable value. Books more than four or five years old are a menace.

OUT OF DATE = DANGEROUS

This offer is to individuals only.

ACKNOWLEDGEMENTS

We are grateful for the advice and suggestions of the following people: Tod Boley, Ron Chase, Jerome Lawson, Carmen Massey, Mark Peppard, and Paul Rosenthal.

NOTE

Doubtless, in your wandering through the mesas and arroyos of T.V.'s horse opera country, you have heard the term "homestead" used to describe certain land laws of the United States allowing settlers to obtain free federal land. This book has absolutely nothing to do with these laws. If your primary interest is in raising a few chickens or perhaps a pig or two on a place of your own, the best advice we can give is to put down this book and go get a Whole Earth Catalogue. But if you are interested in protecting that place of your own so you can raise your chickens with peace of mind, then this book can be of great value.

Table of Contents

CHAPTER 1

General Things

If you own (or are buying) the place you live in, you can protect it from your present and future creditors by simply filing a sample form called a "Homestead." It only costs $4 to file; it's not hard to do, and it gains you great protections and security.

With high levels of unemployment, prices rising almost daily, and ever increasing quantities of consumer goods dangled in front of our eyes on supposedly easy credit terms, many people face financial problems or fear that some unexpected development will cause these problems to arise in the future. We can't in this little book do much to cure the ills of an unhappy society, but we can, at least, show you how to protect your home from most hungry creditors.

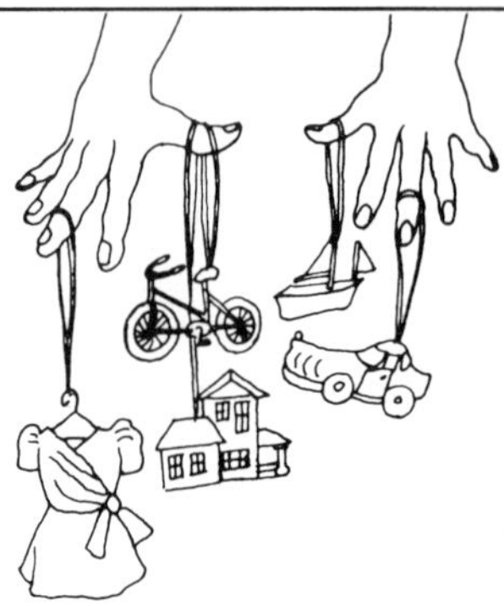

Shortly after the gold rush, the makers of the California Constitution understood that everyone is better off if money lenders can't take away a person's home and throw him and his family out into the cold. They wanted people to have a degree of security in their homes, and not have to live with the fear that some unexpected debt or future creditor might cause them to lose it. They put this notion into the Constitution and left it to the Legislature to make the laws and rules putting it into action.

Although to a certain extent persons are now automatically protected under the Homestead laws, the protection is more complete and gives you greater freedom of action if you have a "Declaration of Homestead" on file prior to the time a judgment is obtained against you.

To protect your home to the maximum extent possible, it is necessary to file a "Declaration of Homestead" and to do so in the proper way. No problem though--just read this book carefully, follow the simple instructions for completing the brief form found at the end of the book, and then file it with your County Recorder. That's all you'll have to do.

When you file a homestead declaration, it is impossible for your creditors to force a sale of your home, unless your debt is for back child support or alimony, or for taxes, or unless the amount of money which could be realized from a sale of your house, after all existing liens, mortgages, and costs of sale have been paid off, is more than the sum protected by the homestead.

Other than these situations, once you have filed your Declaration of Homestead your home cannot be taken to pay off debts no matter what type they are and regardless of whether they were accumulated by accident, misfortune, mismanagement or even plain stupidity. In short, your homestead will drive the wolf (in the guise of a hungry creditor) from your door both now and forever.

NOTE: The existence of the "declared" and "automatic" homesteads with very similar, but not quite identical, provisions is confusing to everyone. Read carefully and you should be able to understand the differences. But be warned. This area of the law was revamped (poorly in our opinion) on July 1, 1983, and there are sure to be more changes once the courts go to work on the changes. The Nolo News, published four times a year by Nolo Press, 950 Parker St., Berkeley, CA 94710 will keep you up to date. Please send $2.00 for the first four issues.

LAWYERS? Lawyers usually charge $50 to $150 to do a homestead for you, but filing a homestead is so simple that almost anyone using this book will be able to do his own. A few persons may find themselves in an unusual or an unclear situation which indicates the need for some legal advice; we have flagged such problem areas here and there throughout this book. At the back, we have included a section on how to choose and use a lawyer, should the need arise. Generally speaking, you will not need a lawyer <u>unless</u>:

a) you finish this book and remain uncertain or confused;

b) you own and live in more than one place and have some doubt as to which is your legal residence;

c) you own a house and are not sure if it is your legal residence;

d) the place you are homesteading is used primarily for business purposes;

e) you want to homestead a long term lease of 30 years or more;

f) you have not homesteaded your house and a creditor is seeking to take it from you (but first see Chapter 10);

g) you face any situation in which a creditor is trying to sell your dwelling, whether or not you have filed a Declaration of Homestead;

h) your home is owned by a corporation rather than by you in your individual capacity;

i) you are not living in your home when a judgment lien is filed against it.

CHAPTER 2

What Is A Homestead?

A. Definitions

DWELLING: Under the homestead laws, dwelling has two different meanings. For the purpose of the "automatic homestead" law (discussed in Chapter 10), a dwelling is any place owned by you where you actually reside, and includes houses (together with the land and any outbuildings), mobile and motor homes, boats, condominiums, planned developments, stock cooperatives and community apartment projects (see Chapter 6 for a more complete discussion of this definition).

For the purpose of declaring a homestead, however, the term "dwelling" only refers to a personally-owned home which is also considered real estate. Thus, for example, houses, condominiums and mobile homes which are permanently placed on land qualify as dwellings for purposes of declaring a homestead, whereas a boat or motor home does not, due to the lack of attached real estate.

REMEMBER: The automatic homestead laws cover virtually any living space, whereas the declared homestead law, which requires that you file a Declaration of Homestead with the County Recorder, only applies to living spaces connected to land.

EQUITY: The amount of your home that you actually own. It is figured by taking the Fair Market Value (which is what you could get for your home if you sold it) and subtracting the costs of sale and the pay-off on any loans secured by the property (in particular the mortgage). For example, if your home could be sold for $80,000 and you owe $57,000 on your mortgage, and it would cost $5,000 to sell it (realtor's commissions, etc.), then your equity is $18,000.

FORCED SALE: This is what happens when you owe money, don't pay it, and your creditor(s) put your home up for sale to get their money.

<u>HOMESTEAD (Automatic)</u>: An automatic homestead protects the dwelling in which a debtor is living from the time a creditor files a judgment lien against the property until the case actually gets to court and a judge approves of the debtor's homestead claim. For example, if a creditor gets a fifty-thousand dollar judgment against Tom and files a judgment lien against Tom's house where he maintains his home, the house qualifies as a homestead, even though Tom has never filed a formal Declaration of Homestead, so long as Tom continues living there up until the time a court determines the homestead to officially exist. However, if Tom is not living in the dwelling when the foreclosure action is brought, or moves out before a judge approves of the homestead, he has no protection at all under the Automatic Homestead Law.

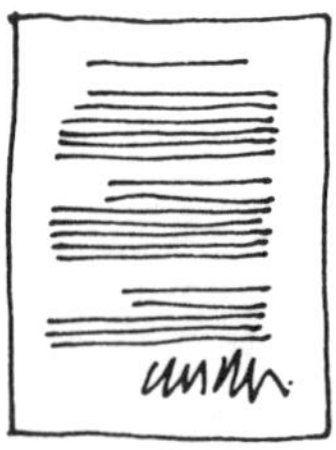

<u>HOMESTEAD (Declared)</u>: This is a written form (see sample at the back of this book) announcing your intent to homestead your property, which, if filed with the County Recorder prior to the filing of a judgment lien by a creditor, protects your property against forced sale and the subsequent imposition of judgment liens, assuming you are living

in it when a judgment lien is filed against your property. Further, in order to obtain such protection, you have to be maintaining the house as your home at the time you file the Declaration of Homestead.

COMPARISON NOTE: Under existing practice, the primary advantage of filing a Declaration of Homestead is that the property can more easily be sold and the proceeds reinvested in another house without having to pay your creditors in the meantime, whereas in the "automatic homestead" situation, the existence of judgment liens may make it extremely difficult to sell without first paying off your debts. This is covered in more detail in Chapter 10. Please understand that this is an evolving area of the law and if your house is being sold to satisfy debts, you should check any information you read here to be sure it is current.

JUDGMENT CREDITOR: In this context, any person or entity who has recovered a judgment in a California court against the person whose home is being homesteaded.

JUDGMENT LIENS: By filing a copy of a court judgment against you with the County Recorder, a creditor can automatically place a claim (termed a lien) on your property, which must usually be paid off if and when your house is sold. By filing a Declaration of Homestead, you will usually prevent the judgments from operating as liens and will thus be able to sell your property and reinvest in another home without having to first satisfy the filed judgments. However, there are several exceptions to this protection, such as materialman's liens, which are discussed later, in Chapter 10.

B. Amount of Equity Protected

The amount of equity protected by a homestead is not unlimited. The Legislature adjusts it upwards from time to time, but as of the writing of this book, the protection is as follows:*

If you are:	Then your equity is protected up to:
a single person	$30,000
a married couple	$45,000
a single person who qualifies as head of family**	$45,000
either you (or your spouse) is over 65	$55,000
either you (or your spouse) is disabled***	$55,000

---

* The legislature has periodically adjusted the amounts of these exemptions upwards. New homestead exemption levels apply to all Declarations of Homestead previously filed, except that protection for contractual debts (i.e., installment sales, bank loans, etc.) is measured by the exemption in effect when the debt is incurred. Debts incurred after the increase are subject to the increased exemption. Debts arising from personal injuries, however, are always subject to the latest exemption level, at least according to one court case. INGEBRETSEN V. MCNAMER 137 Cal.App.3d 957.

** This can be any single individual who has a dependent close relative under his or her care and maintenance and who resides on the premises.

*** Disabled individuals include those receiving Social Security Disability or SSI benefits and others who are incapable of substantial gainful employment.

✓ <u>NOTE:</u> As of this printing the $55,000 exemption for elderly and disabled persons is expected to increase to $60,000, effective January 1, 1987. Final word on this will appear in the November issue of the *Nolo News*. Call Nolo Press for a complimentary copy. In any case, if the new amount is approved it will automatically raise the exemption for everyone in that category no matter when the homestead was filed.

If you own equity in excess of the amount protected, your creditors may be able to reach it. This is discussed in detail in Section E, below. It's possible to reduce your equity to keep it within the protected amount by refinancing the place, taking out another loan on it, etc. A lawyer or accountant might have some bright ideas on the subject and ought to be consulted before you act.

<u>IMPORTANT</u>: Immediately after you file your homestead, you should write to your State Senator and Assemblyman. Tell them that considering the current price of housing, the least they could do would be to increase the amount of equity protected by the homestead (see Appendix C).

C. Debts Not Covered by Homestead

A homestead (either automatic or declared) will protect your home from being sold to satisfy the great majority of your debts. It makes no difference if the debt is to the butcher, dressmaker, doctor, furniture store, airline, or was incurred as a result of an automobile accident--you are protected.

The following kinds of debts are not covered by either an "automatic" or "declared" homestead:

1. Child Support and Alimony: The homestead laws do not protect your home against judgments obtained for back child support or alimony obligations. The reason for this is the strong social policy in favor of making sure these obligations are met.

2. Deed of Trust and Mortgage: The homestead laws do not protect your property against being sold to satisfy loans secured by the property itself. These type of loans, commonly called Deeds of Trust, Second Deeds of Trust, and Mortgages, are exempt from the Homestead laws for the obvious reason that no creditor would lend you money in the first place unless they could sell your home if you didn't make your payments. The lesson here is, homestead laws don't keep the wolf from your door when it is holding a mortgage or second deed of trust in its jaw.

CAUTION: Most places have a mortgage or a trust deed as part of the original purchase transaction, but you should try very hard not to put your place up as security for any other loans, unless you have thought it out very carefully ahead of time, and absolutely need to. Some unscrupulous lenders or people who sell goods on installment contracts have been known to trick people into putting up their home as security without their actually knowing it. When borrowing money or buying things on time, be sure to read the contract very carefully to make sure that you do not carelessly or unintentionally sign away your place as security for a loan.

3. Taxes: Your government is perfectly willing to protect you from other greedy creditors, but not when it comes to its own bill--it thinks there's some-

thing very sacred about the money you owe the government in the form of taxes. If you can't pay your tax bills, then you should know that local and county governments are usually quite slow to act, and reasonable about helping you out, but watch out for the feds.* The IRS has been known to act rather heartlessly.

<u>MATERIALMAN'S LIEN NOTE</u>: When materialman's liens are filed against a house with a declared homestead, a sale cannot be forced. However, the liens will have to be paid if the property is voluntarily sold. See Chapter 10.

* It normally takes five years for city and county governments to move to sell your house for non-payment of taxes. Under the Senior Citizens Property Tax Postponement Act, many homeowners age 62 or over can postpone property taxes until death or sale of the house. Contact the Franchise Tax Board for more information.

D. Law Suit? It's Still Not Too Late

Often people think of getting a homestead only when their debts are piled up, or when someone sues them. It is still not too late to file a Declaration of Homestead on your place at this stage. However, in order for you to take advantage of the extra protections offered by the Declared Homestead (see Chapter 10), it must be filed before your creditor actually obtains a judgment from a court and files it with the County Recorder.

For example, suppose you become involved in a dispute over a defective used T.V. which you recently purchased from your neighborhood T.V. bargain shop. If you refuse to pay for it, the person (creditor) must first sue you, get a judgment from a court, and then record a copy of the judgment with the County Recorder before your wages and property can be snatched to pay for the T.V. If by the time the judgment is recorded you still have not gotten around to filing your Declaration of Homestead, then it's too late. What's the moral? At, or preferably before, the time you are first sued, make sure you file a Declaration of Homestead. You are still protected by the automatic homestead, however, if you file a claim of exemption. If a judgment has been entered against you and a lien has been filed against your home, filing a claim of exemption will give you considerable protection, but not as much as if you had properly filed your Declaration of Homestead (see Chapter 1Ø).

E. Sale by Creditors to Reach Excess Equity

If you have an equity in your home larger than the homestead protection, then your creditors can, in theory, act to have your house sold.*

---

* California Code of Civil Procedure (C.C.P.) Section 7Ø4.8ØØ. For an outline of what is involved in getting a homesteaded house sold against the owner's will, see C.C.P. Section 7Ø4.75Ø.

However, any judgment creditor who wants to enforce a judgment on a homestead involving real property (i.e., houses, condominiums, cooperatives, and mobilehomes permanently situated on land) must first apply to the proper court for the issuance of a writ of execution.* The creditor's application must state 1) whether a declared homestead on the property is currently on file and if so in whose name and in what amount, and 2) the amount of any liens on the property and the address of the lien holders.

Once the application is filed with the court, the court will issue a document called an "Order to Show Cause," which basically gives the property owner a chance to come into court and present her views about whether the property should be sold.** The form which you will receive giving you notice of the

---

* This application process does not apply where your homestead consists of "personal" property such as a boat, motor home, or mobile home which is transportable. In such cases, you will need to file a claim of exemption in order to claim your homestead. This process is described in Chapter 11.

** C.C.P Section 704.770(a).

hearing will look like this:

9-26.1

SHORT TITLE	LEVYING OFFICER FILE NO	COURT CASE NO

NOTICE

IMPORTANT LEGAL NOTICE TO HOMEOWNER

1. **YOUR HOME IS ABOUT TO BE SOLD TO PAY OFF YOUR DEBTS.**
2. **YOU MAY BE ABLE TO STOP THE SALE OR KEEP SOME OF THE MONEY FROM THE SALE. Before your home is sold, the court will have a hearing to let you prove that you or your family live there. YOU OR YOUR SPOUSE SHOULD COME TO THIS HEARING.**

DATE, TIME, AND PLACE OF THE HEARING

Date:
Time:
Place:*

3. **READ THE PAPERS THAT CAME WITH THIS NOTICE. At the hearing you will be asked about the statements in those papers.**
4. **The only purpose of the hearing is to decide if your home should be sold and if you qualify for a homestead exemption on the money from the sale. The purpose is NOT to decide if you owe the debts. That has already been decided.**
5. **You are not required to bring an attorney with you to the hearing. For your own protection, you may want to ask an attorney for advice right away.**
6. **If you do not own this home, this notice is not for you. PLEASE GIVE THIS NOTICE TO YOUR LANDLORD IMMEDIATELY.**

AVISO

AVISO LEGAL IMPORTANTE PARA EL PROPIETARIO DE CASA

1. **SU CASA ESTA A PUNTO DE VENDERSE PARA PAGAR SUS DEUDAS.**
2. **USTED PUEDE DETENER LA VENTA O RECIBIR PARTE DEL DINERO DE LA VENTA. Antes de la venta de su casa, habrá una audiencia en la corte para permitirle que pruebe que usted o su familia vive allí. USTED O SU CONYUGE DEBE ASISTIR A LA AUDIENCIA.**

FECHA, HORA Y LUGAR DE LA AUDIENCIA

Fecha *(date)*:
Hora *(time)*:
Lugar *(place)*:*

3. **LEA LOS DOCUMENTOS QUE LLEGARON CON ESTE AVISO. En la audiencia se le harán preguntas relacionadas con las declaraciones contenidas en estos documentos.**
4. **La audiencia tiene solamente el propósito de decidir si su casa debe venderse y si usted es elegible a la exención de bienes de familia sobre el dinero de la venta. La audiencia NO es para decidir si usted es responsable de las deudas. Esto ya fue decidido.**
5. **Usted no está obligado a venir a la audiencia con un abogado. Para su propia protección, es posible que usted quiera consultar con un abogado de inmediato.**
6. **Si usted no es el propietário de esta casa, este aviso no es para usted. POR FAVOR, ENTREGUESELO INMEDIATAMENTE A SU ARRENDADOR.**

*Specify location from Order to Show Cause

Form Approved by the Judicial Council of California EJ-180 (New January 1, 1985)

NOTICE OF HEARING ON RIGHT TO HOMESTEAD EXEMPTION
(Enforcement of Judgment)

CCP 704.770

At the court hearing, if there is a declared homestead on file, it's up to the creditor to convince the court that the homestead is invalid in order to get the property sold on that ground.* This is virtually impossible to do unless there is some major defect in the homestead declaration.

If there is no declared homestead, the debtor has to prove that the property is protected by the automatic homestead provision.** This may not be too difficult, but this time the "burden of proof" is on the debtor. For example, supposing your creditor claims you were not really a resident in the dwelling. If there is a Declaration of Homestead on file the creditor would have to prove

* C.C.P. Section 704.780(a).

** C.C.P. Section 704.780(a).

his allegation by bringing in evidence. Conversely, if there is no declaration on file, and the creditor claims a lack of a homestead in the property, you might have to bring in some witnesses showing that you were living there when the judgment lien was filed with the court clerk.

If the application for the forced sale states the amount of the homestead exemption as being one figure (say $30,000), but the debtor believes that it's higher ($45,000 or $55,000), then the debtor must establish that fact, whether the homestead is "automatic" or "declared."*

After these basics are taken care of, the judge must determine the fair market value of the property, with the help of an appraiser if necessary, and then if he finds that either there is no homestead protection or the equity in the dwelling is more than the homestead, he must order the property sold.**

However, just because the property is ordered sold doesn't mean it will be. When homesteaded property (either automatic or declared) is subjected to a forced sale, the sale cannot go through unless a bid is received which is higher than a) the amount of the homestead ($55,000, $45,000 or $30,000) plus b) the amount necessary to satisfy all existing liens and encumbrances, including but not limited to, any attachment or judgment liens).***

---

* C.C.P. Section 704.780(a)(2).

** C.C.P. Section 704.780(b) & (d).

***C.C.P. Section 704.800(a).

REMEMBER: Homesteaded property cannot be forcibly sold unless the amount received will provide the homestead holder with at least the amount of the applicable homestead exemption, free and clear. If such a bid is not received, then the court order is cancelled and the property cannot be placed for sale for at least another year.* Also, if the bid is not at least 90% of the fair market value as determined by the judge, the creditor has an option of either rejecting the offer or asking for a new sale order.**

* C.C.P. Section 704.800(a).

** C.C.P. Section 704.800(b).

SUMMARY: Let's take a look and see where we are. The Homestead law automatically provides you with a cash value protection on your home if you're living in it when a judgment against you is filed with the County Recorder's Office. However, if the amount of the debt is more than the homestead protection amount added to all the liens and encumbrances on the property, the property can be forcibly sold to meet the debt. In such a case, you will receive your Homestead amount from the sale. In the case of real estate types of dwellings, the creditor must apply to the court to authorize the sale, whereas in the case of personal property types of dwellings (boats, motor homes, etc.), you will need to file a claim of exemption (see Chapter 11).

If you have filed a Declaration of Homestead before the judgment is filed with the County Recorder's Office, you are subject to the same procedure. But you will be able to sell the house and retain the exemption amount for investment in another dwelling. See Chapter 9.

EXAMPLE: Your family home is homesteaded; it is worth $97,000 and has a $20,000 first mortgage and a $5,000 second mortgage on it. If a creditor gets a judgment which you don't pay, he can act to have your place sold. But this means that he must pay off the $25,000 in mortgages, and pay to you the $45,000 covered by your homestead. Out of the remaining money ($27,ØØØ if the house is sold for its full value), he must pay the legal, appraisal and selling costs--a considerable sum, most likely. In the example above, the creditor might well choose to go ahead with the sale, whereas if the house were worth much less, all else being the same, the creditor would probably not find it worthwhile, as the costs would eat up anything he could hope to receive. He also knows that he's not likely to get market value for the house at a forced sale.

NOTE: If you have equity in excess of the protected amount, and if you are concerned about your creditors, then you can possibly reduce your equity in your place by borrowing more money on it.

Notice that even if your home with a declared homestead gets sold you get a bundle of cash, whereas if it was not

homesteaded, you may get nothing in some circumstances (see Chapter 10 for automatic homestead information).

NOTE: Even if you, your spouse, or your attorney did not appear at the first hearing, and the judge issued a writ of execution, you still get a second chance if the failure to appear was due to mistake, excusable neglect, inadvertance, or surprise. If this has happened to you, you'll need to execute a declaration saying why you defaulted and give it to the sheriff, who in turn will give it the judge, who in turn will schedule a hearing to see whether you deserve another chance. The law really does go out of its way to make sure you're not deprived of any homestead to which you might otherwise be entitled.

If you did miss the first hearing, we recommend you see an attorney about helping you get your second chance. What constitutes mistake, excusable neglect, inadvertance or surprise is hard to determine in any particular situation and may depend on the judge hearing the case.

CHAPTER 3

What Does It Do To My "Credit?"

If a wise man were required to give away his possessions in their order of importance, so that he shed the least important first, he would certainly get rid of his good credit rating at the start. After all, what is a good credit rating other than a license to buy lots of things you can do without, at prices that exceed their true worth to you, while paying unreasonable amounts of interest for the privilege. Clearly, it makes much better sense to buy less in the first place, and always to buy only those things that you can easily and conveniently afford.

Some people may tell you that putting a homestead on your place hurts your credit rating. This is not true. In most cases, the person extending credit depends upon the borrower's ability to repay, and does not rely on the possibility of selling his house to collect the bill. To sell the house is so much trouble, and so time consuming, that any fairly intelligent, reputable lender would want to avoid such a route. Reputable lenders make a good living selling quality goods or lending their money to good credit risks. They do not need to resort to selling a person's house. However, there are a lot of lenders who feel differently, such as those in the business of second-mortgage lending.

For a few people, a homestead may damage an already bad credit rating. These are people who are so marginal economically that no one would lend them money without the prospect of collecting by foreclosing on their house. This is just exactly the group of persons who should avoid credit buying like it was the plague. You simply don't want to buy on time when some high-pressure car or appliance salesman is already eyeing the color of your bedroom wallpaper.

CHAPTER 4

Residency Requirement

The person filing a homestead declaration must reside in the place being homesteaded.

For most people, this will be no problem. It is usually simple to tell where you reside--it's the place where you live and intend to go on living for the indefinite future. Some people may be away a lot, or spend summers and vacations in a country home, and still have a primary place of residence which can be homesteaded. Domestic problems may result in one or the other spouse being temporarily forced out of the home to which he or she intends to return. Such a temporary absence should not jeopardize his or her homestead rights. If you have any real doubt as to where you reside, see a lawyer. You should

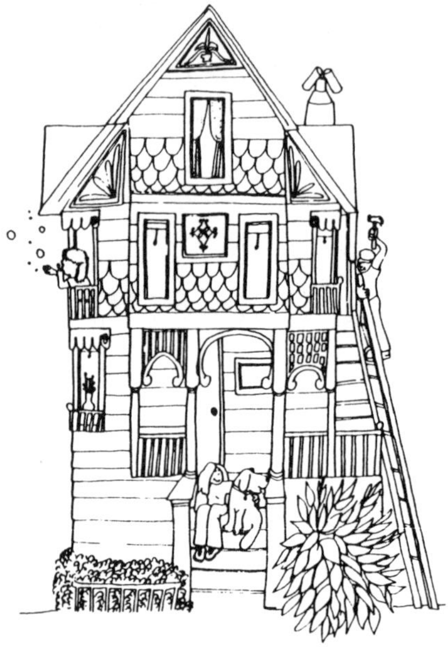

definitely see a lawyer if you live in more than one place and are not sure which is your primary place of residence, if you are away from your home most of the time, or if you don't have a present intention to live in the place you want to homestead.

NOTE: Remember, even though you have a Declaration of Homestead on file, you need to be living in your dwelling at the time a judgment is filed against it. Otherwise, your Declaration won't be worth a plugged nickel.

CHAPTER 5

Who May File A Homestead?

Anyone who is buying (or owns) the place he is living in can file a Declaration of Homestead. (In fact, several persons can file separate homesteads on the same property so long as each person owns part of it. Thus, three individuals living together, each owning a one-third interest in the property, could each file a separate homestead to protect his or her share. However, only individuals are allowed homestead protection. Corporations do not qualify.)

While the homestead law is intended to protect ownership interests in a dwelling, it does provide for different amounts, depending on who is living there when foreclosure is sought (i.e., when the judge is asked by the creditor to have the dwelling sold.

Amounts of Homestead Protection

When one owner is listed on the Declaration of Homestead or living in the dwelling at the time the homestead is automatically applied (see Chapter 10), and that owner is not yet 65 years old or disabled, the exemption is $30,000.

When a single owner is part of a family unit, as that term is defined in the law, the homestead protection is $45,000.

"Family units" include any of the following living situations which exist at the time the court considers whether the dwelling should be sold:

1. The judgment debtor and spouse if the two are residing together;

2. The judgment debtor and any of the following persons who the judgment debtor cares for or maintains in the homestead, (assuming that these other persons either have no ownership in the house or only own a community property interest);

a. The minor child or minor grandchild of the judgment debtor or the judgment debtor's spouse or the minor child or grandchild of a deceased spouse or former spouse;

b. The minor brother or sister of the judgment debtor or judgment debtor's spouse or the minor child of a deceased brother or sister of either spouse;

c. The father, mother, grandfather, or grandmother of the judgment debtor or the judgment debtor's spouse or the father, mother, grandfather, or grandmother of a deceased spouse;

d. An unmarried relative described in this list who has attained the age of majority and is unable to take care of or support himself or herself; or

3. The judgment debtor's spouse and at least one of the persons listed in items a through d above who the judgment debtor's spouse cares for or maintains in the homestead.*

Roughly summarized, the homestead exemption is $45,000 if the dwelling is inhabited at the right time by the judgment debtor and her spouse, or by one of them and anyone from the list set out above.

If the judgment debtor or spouse of the judgment debtor is either over 65 years of age or is unable to engage in substantial gainful employment at the time the property is to be sold, the homestead protection is $55,000.** Persons are presumed to be disabled if they are receiving social security disability or SSI benefits. However, others may establish their disability as well.

---

* C.C.P. Section 704.710(b).

** Expected to increase to $60,000, effective January 1, 1987.

UNRELATED FAMILY NOTE: It is clear that the legislature only intends the $45,000 exemption to apply to families related by blood or marriage. Thus, even if your living arrangement is "family" in every sense of the word, if no one of the specified relatives of the home's owner is living there, the exemption is only $30,000. However, if one or more unrelated persons are living together and each is an owner, each may independently declare a $30,000 homestead on his or her ownership share. And, if these persons are over 65 or disabled, this amount may be $55,000 each. Simply put, two unmarried people may get better protection than a married couple.

CHANGED CIRCUMSTANCES NOTE: Subsequent to January 1, 1985, the amount of protection available under a Declared Homestead depends on who is living there when a sale is attempted. Prior to that time, the level of protection depended upon the status claimed in the Declaration. Although it now appears that you need not file a new Declaration in order to obtain greater protection than your filed Declaration indicates, this point has not yet been addressed by the courts. We therefore suggest that you file a new Declaration whenever you are entitled to more protection than your Declaration on file would suggest.

Because your birthdate (and that of your spouse) is on the Declaration, you need not file a new Declaration to obtain the increased protection for persons over 65. However, if you move from a single person to a family unit situation, or you or your spouse become disabled, a new Declaration is definitely in order.

There is an additional important reason for keeping your Declaration current. Suppose a judgment-creditor examines your Declaration in order to decide whether to attempt a forced sale of your home. If the Declaration shows you are entitled to an exemption of $45,000 or $55,000, the creditor may decide not to bother, whereas a Declaration showing a $30,000 exemption might encourage the creditor to proceed.

CHAPTER 6

What Kinds of Property Are Protected?

You may file a Declaration of Homestead in respect to almost any real estate you own or are buying so long as you use it as your primary residence at the time of filing. It can be a place in the country, a house in the city, a condominium, cooperative apartment or planned unit development, or even a mobile home, if it is permanently situated on land. The homestead includes all the land you own, as well as the house and disconnected outbuildings such as garages, guest cottages or tool sheds. In this book, whenever we refer to your house, home, place or property, that includes any or all of the above.

HOME AND BUSINESS COMBINED? Sometimes your house is more than just a home, but this probably won't invalidate your homestead. In an older case, California courts held that a woman running a prostitution operation in her home was eligible to declare a homestead, but in another case they held that a man living in the back of his small factory was not. More recently, courts have become liberal in allowing homesteads on property where business is being conducted, so long as it is also the bona fide residence of the individual or family declaring the homestead. In the case of VIOTTI V. GIOMI, the court said:

> The use of a building partly or even chiefly for business purposes or the renting of part of it is not inconsistent with the right of a homestead provided it is and continues to be the bona fide residence of the family.

Thus, if you live in your own small apartment building or rooming house, or if your front room is a beauty shop or an office, or if you make leather purses at home, you can still file a homestead declaration. On the other hand, if you sleep in a broom closet in the back of a gas station, you probably could not homestead the place. The test seems to be whether or not the residence is bona fide, and not whether the business activity is more extensive than the use of the place as a home. If your own situation is unclear in the light of this discussion, be sure to consult a lawyer before filing.

CORPORATION NOTE: Remember that homestead protection only applies to ownership by individuals and not profit, non-profit or professional corporations.

CHAPTER 7

More Than One Homestead?

You are only entitled to declare a homestead on one dwelling at a time. For example, let's say that you filed a homestead on your old place, then later you moved out but still own it. Years have passed, and you now want to file on your present place. When you do, the law will automatically consider your prior homestead to have been abandoned as to you and your interest in your former property will no longer be protected.* However, if both you and your spouse were listed on the prior Declaration of Homestead, and she still lives there, her interest will continue to be protected under the prior declaration.

If you sell your homesteaded property, the homestead is also automatically

* C.C.P. Section 704.990.

extinguished as to your interest. For example, suppose you are a part owner of property on which you declared a $30,000 homestead for your interest. If you sell your share to somebody else, only your homestead will be cancelled and any other Declaration of Homestead filed by the other owners will not be affected by your sale.

Even though your prior homestead is automatically abandoned when you sell your interest in the property or file a Declaration of Homestead on another piece of property, you are also entitled to explicitly abandon it by filing a Declaration of Abandonment (see the Form and Instructions in Appendix C). This abandonment will only operate in respect to the person making it, the same as when the abandonment takes place automatically.*

---

* C.C.P. Section 704.980.

CHAPTER 8

Death, Divorce and Bankruptcy

A Declaration of Homestead is a property protection, and can create a property right. There are some practical consequences of making the homestead declaration that you should know about. This is not a law text, so we do not go into details, but we can discuss the practical effects of your homestead in general terms. If, after you read this, you feel that you have a problem or confusion in any one of these areas, you should consult an attorney. For most folks, however, it's all pretty straightforward.

Apart from protecting you from hungry creditors, the times that a homestead has consequences are in the event of a death, divorce or bankruptcy. Sale of the homesteaded property is discussed separately in the next chapter.

A. Death

When someone dies, their property is disposed of according to their will unless they have placed the dwelling in joint tenancy, an intervivos trust, or other probate avoidance device. If they leave no will and make no other provision for their property, it goes according to law. This means it passes first to a surviving spouse, but if there is no spouse, then to the children, and if no children, then to other relatives in various orders of preference. This can often get a little complicated and it is essential that you do some advance planning. The best source of information for the non-lawyer in this area is Denis Clifford's PLAN YOUR ESTATE WITH WILLS, PROBATE AVOIDANCE, TRUSTS AND TAXES (see back of this book for details).

Here are some general rules that apply when one or more owner(s) of a declared homestead dies:

- If one joint owner of a dwelling dies and the other(s) has previously independently declared a homestead on his or her interest in the property, that interest is still protected;

- Any surviving spouse or other member of the deceased homestead owner's family will be protected under the homestead declaration providing: 1) they are living in the dwelling at the time the homestead owner dies, and 2) they inherit all or part of the deceased owner's interest in the dwelling. This is true even though the surviving person was not listed in the Declaration of Homestead;*

- If a property owner with a declared homestead dies and the property is left to someone other than a spouse who was included in the homestead declaration, the new owner is not protected until he or she moves into the dwelling and files his or her own homestead.

There is also something in California law called a "probate homestead."** A probate homestead is created by the court for the purpose of providing shelter for surviving family members while

---

* C.C.P. Section 704.995

** Probate Code Section 660.

the estate of the deceased person is being settled. It is not the same thing as the Declaration of Homestead discussed in this book and does not depend on filing any papers with the County Recorder's Office such as the ones at the end of this book.

In deciding whether to establish a probate homestead, the court has wide discretion to decide whether to set apart property (including the family home) to the surviving spouse and/or to the minor child(ren). Any action on the part of the court is not likely to occur for about five months after the death of the property owner. This is because until the inventory of the estate is filed with the court (within three months after appointment of an executor) and for sixty days after that, the widow(er) and minor child(ren) are automatically entitled to continue to own and occupy their home. In addition, the clothing of the family, household furniture and other property of the deceased spouse are completely exempt from being taken to satisfy the debts of the deceased.

When deciding whether it should set apart a probate homestead, the judge considers if the property could have been homesteaded during the lifetime of the deceased spouse and whether it is suitable for residential purposes; the rights of the creditors; the estate's financial status; the value of the homestead; as well as the situation of the surviving family.

If the spouse remarries and/or if the children reach majority, the court will not set apart a probate homestead.

B. Divorce

A divorce ends any right that one spouse has in the homesteaded property of the other. Separate property always belongs to its owner, and the homestead gave the other spouse no ownership interest in it.

A divorce does not, in and of itself alone, end a community homestead interest. People can get a divorce and yet continue to own property together if they so choose. In order to end a homestead interest in community property, you need to transfer the property from one spouse to the other. This is normally done by a grant deed or quitclaim deed. In the divorce process, the judge will normally order that one spouse or the other will get the property, then he'll order both parties to sign any necessary papers to make the transfer, or if a legal description of the property is set forth in the divorce decree, he can order the decree itself filed with the County Recorder. If you choose to have some other arrangement, you should make a property settlement agreement prior to going into court.*

* This is covered in our book by Charles Sherman, HOW TO DO YOUR OWN DIVORCE IN CALIFORNIA.

If a couple owned a community homestead which, for some reason, was not transferred by deed after a divorce, then the declared homestead continues to be valid, assuming one of the two spouses is living in the home at the time a creditor tries to have the home sold.

C. Bankruptcy

Each year thousands of Californians find it necessary or useful to declare bankruptcy. Indeed, as our economy becomes more and more bizarre, and as merchants heedlessly extend credit to almost anyone, without regard to their ability to pay, the number of bankruptcies increases. If you've been playing the game of life, are way out on a limb with too many bills and not enough income, and you want to learn your lesson and start over, you can file bankruptcy. If you have a homestead you won't lose your house.

If you own a home and decide to declare bankruptcy, the equity in the home is protected up to the appropriate exemption amount (discussed in Chapter 2) and cannot be taken by the bankruptcy court to pay bills. This assumes, however, that the judgment debtor or spouse is living in the home, and is true whether or not a Declaration of Homestead has been filed or the automatic exemption is being relied on.

NOTE: The best source of information for those over their heads in debt and facing lawsuits, attachments, bill collector harrassment and the possibility of bankruptcy is THE CALIFORNIA DEBTOR'S HANDBOOK--BILLPAYERS' RIGHTS, by Warner & Honigsberg, BANKRUPTCY: DO IT YOURSELF and CHAPTER 13: THE FEDERAL PLAN TO REPAY YOUR DEBTS, both by Janice Kosel. These books can be ordered from Nolo Press by following the instructions at the back of this book.

CHAPTER 9

Selling The Homesteaded Home

In our ever more mobile society, it is becoming normal to buy a house, live in it for a few years, and then move on. If you sell your property, or it is sold involuntarily, the declared homestead law not only protects a certain amount of your equity (i.e., between $30,000 and $55,000), but also gives you six months to find another house before creditors can grab the proceeds.* Unfortunately, if you are relying on the automatic homestead provisions, you may have a problem getting your money out of the first house and into the second without paying off the judgment liens. This is because title companies may refuse to clear title unless you have a declared homestead or pay off the liens. If you find yourself in this situation,

* C.C.P. Sections 704.20, 704.960.

a consultation with a lawyer is advisable. Also, if you are relying on the automatic homestead provision and you and your spouse are living in separate homes, only one of you will be able to use this protection,* whereas if each of you has a declared homestead on your separate homes, each of you is protected for the six month period.

When you sell (transfer title to) a home, you automatically abandon any homestead you might have on it.

If one spouse conveys homesteaded property to the other, the spouse making the conveyance (selling out) abandons all homestead interest in the property unless he or she specifically reserves homestead rights.

---

* C.C.P. Section 704.720(c).

CHAPTER 10

Protecting Your Home Without A Homestead

As we have mentioned in previous chapters, you have a certain amount of protection of the equity in your home as a matter of law, whether or not you actually take the step of filing a Declaration of Homestead. We've stressed, however, that there are advantages to filing the Declaration. Here are the main ones:

- Any surviving spouse or other member of the deceased homestead owner's family will be protected under the homestead declaration providing 1) they are living in the dwelling at the time the homestead owner dies and 2) they inherit all or part of the deceased owner's interest in the dwelling. This is true even though the surviving person was not listed in the Declaration of Homestead.

- When a Declaration of Homestead has been filed, the law prevents judgment liens from being filed against the property (except judgments for child support, alimony and taxes) unless the amount of the lien is greater than the total of existing liens and encumbrances and the homestead exemption amount. In most cases, therefore, filing the Declaration keeps liens off your property. This is important if you want to sell it, since title companies will usually not establish clear title unless and until all liens are paid off. In other words, by filing a Declaration of Homestead you can sell your home and put the proceeds in a new one (within six months) without having to use the proceeds to pay off existing judgments. The automatic homestead exemption, on the other hand, does not prevent the filing of judgment liens against your home and if you want to voluntarily sell your house, you'll very likely have to pay them off first.

- If spouses who have a declared homestead split up and then live in separate dwellings with declared homesteads on them, each can sell their respective dwellings and reinvest the proceeds in new dwellings (so long as they do it within six months) even though they remain married. However, if spouses separate and then live in undeclared homesteads, only one is entitled the automatic homestead protection (see Chapter 9).

- If a creditor tries to force a sale, the person with the declared homestead has an easier time in court since the Declaration of Homestead shifts the burden of proof onto the creditor if the creditor is contending that the homestead is not valid. If the debtor only relies on the automatic homestead provision, however, he or she must assume the burden of proof.

- If your debts leading to a judgment were incurred prior to July 1, 1975, the automatic homestead provisions may not protect you, whereas a Declaration of Homestead would. For most of you, this will not be a problem, but if you have some old debts which might end up in the form of judgments you would be very wise to file a Declaration of Homestead as soon as possible.

In sum, there are advantages to having filed a Declaration of Homestead in the event one or more creditors try to grab your home to pay off a judgment. Still, even if you haven't filed a declaration, remember that you will most often be able to claim the automatic homestead anyway.

MATERIALMAN'S LIEN NOTE: In most cases, a creditor must obtain a judgment in order to place a lien on your property. However, people who do repairs on your house are entitled to file liens against your property (called Mechanic's or Materialman's liens) without first going to court. This means that even if you have a declared homestead, you may have trouble selling your house and reinvesting the proceeds without first paying these debts, since the declared homestead only keeps judgment liens from attaching to your property (except in respect to any amount over your homestead amount and other existing liens and encumbrances).

CHAPTER 11

Housetrailers, Mobile Homes, Houseboats, Etc.

Your ownership equity in almost any type of living space is protected in California by the automatic homestead provisions. Specifically, the law provides that anything used as a dwelling is subject to the automatic homestead protections and gives as examples boats, other "waterborne vessels," and mobile homes. Treehouses, Winnebagos and abandoned railroad cars would also qualify if they were actually being used as your primary residence. However, the fact that the homestead is called automatic does not mean that you can sit back and do nothing.

If your residence is a boat, motorhome, etc., it is considered "personal property," and the burden is on you to take affirmative steps to claim your "automatic" homestead (unlike homes that are considered real property--see Chapter 2). Also, there is no protection against the property being sold, as there is with real property. However, it is unlikely to be sold unless the probable sale amount were in excess of your exemption, costs of sale and existing encumbrances and liens.

If a creditor gets a judgment against you, his next step is to get a "writ of execution" from the court clerk. He then tells the sheriff or marshal to attach your wages, bank account and/or some item of your property.* Let's assume that the creditor wants to sell your houseboat. The sheriff shows up on the dock with the writ of execution and proceeds to seize your home with the purpose of selling it to pay off the judgment debt. This is where you must take action. Under C.C.P. Section 703.520, you are entitled to at least get your homestead amount out of the sale if you file a paper called a "claim of exemption" within 10 days to compel the return of the boat because it is exempt under the homestead law (specifically, C.C.P. Sections 704.710, 704.720, 704.730, and 704.800).

---

* For a full discussion of the attachment procedure as regards wages, bank accounts, and other types of property, such as motor vehicles, and what you can do to protect yourself, see THE CALIFORNIA DEBTOR'S HANDBOOK--BILLPAYERS' RIGHTS, Warner & Honigsberg (order information at back of this book).

Once you fill out the "claim of exemption" and deliver it to the sheriff who seized your home in the first place, the sheriff will deliver the claim to the creditor who must then set up a court hearing, about which you will be given notice, to determine whether you are entitled to your exemption. The burden of proof will be on you to show that the item (a boat in this example) is your principal residence and that you are either entitled to up to $30,000 or $45,000, depending on your status as we discussed in Chapter 5.

A valid claim of exemption must contain the following information:

- The name and mailing address of the claimant;

- The name and mailing address of the judgment debtor if the claimant is not the judgment debtor (i.e., if your boat is mistakenly seized to meet the debts of a former tenant, you need to provide what information you have about the whereabouts of the tenant);

- A description of the property;*

- A reference to the statutes on which your claim is based (these references are given earlier in this chapter);

- A statement of the facts entitling you to the claim (i.e., that you and/or others are using the boat as your principal residence now and at the time the judgment was filed with the County Recorder, that you and/or others own the boat, and that you are entitled to a homestead exemption in the amount of your equity, up to the appropriate limit.

A suggested form and accompanying instructions for you to use are shown on the following pages. You will need at least two copies in addition to the original. The original and one copy must be delivered to the sheriff or

---

* A simple description of the property is sufficient. Here are some examples: (1) My 1963 Roadway Mobilehome (serial #27423) in which I reside; (2) My Seasprite catamaran, docked at slip #13, Alameda, CA., in which I reside.

marshal, and one copy should be retained for your records.

MCF # 117 b 7/83

[NOT FOR WAGE GARNISHMENT]
[RETURN TO LEVYING OFFICER. DO NOT FILE WITH COURT]

ATTORNEY OR PARTY WITHOUT ATTORNEY *(Name and Address)*: (1) TELEPHONE NO.:	LEVYING OFFICER *(Name and Address)*: (5)
ATTORNEY FOR *(Name)*:	
NAME OF COURT, JUDICIAL DISTRICT OR BRANCH COURT, IF ANY: (2)	
PLAINTIFF: (3)	
DEFENDANT: (4)	
CLAIM OF EXEMPTION (Enforcement of Judgment)	LEVYING OFFICER FILE NO.: (6) COURT CASE NO.:

Copy all the information required above (except the top left space) from the Notice of Levy. The top left space is for your name or your attorney's name and address. The original and one copy of this form must be filed with the levying officer. DO NOT FILE WITH THE COURT. (7)

1. My name is *(specify)*:
2. Papers should be sent to
   (8) → ☐ me.
   ☐ my attorney (I have filed with the court and served on the judgment creditor a request that papers be sent to my attorney and my attorney has consented in writing on the request to receive these papers.)
   (9) → at the address ☐ shown above ☐ following *(specify)*:
3. (10) ☐ I am not the judgment debtor named in the notice of levy. The name and last known address of the judgment debtor is *(specify)*:
4. The property I claim to be exempt is *(describe)*: (11)
5. The property is claimed to be exempt under the following code and section *(specify)*: (12)
6. The facts which support this claim are *(describe)*: (13)
7. ☐ The claim is made pursuant to a provision exempting property to the extent necessary for the support of the judgment debtor and the spouse and dependents of the judgment debtor. **A Financial Statement form is attached to this claim.**
8. ☐ The property claimed to be exempt is
   a. ☐ a motor vehicle, the proceeds of an execution sale of a motor vehicle, or the proceeds of insurance or other indemnification for the loss, damage, or destruction of a motor vehicle.
   b. ☐ tools, implements, materials, uniforms, furnishings, books, equipment, a commercial motor vehicle, a vessel, or other personal property used in the trade, business or profession of the judgment debtor or spouse.
   c. all other property of the same type owned by the judgment debtor, either alone or in combination with others, is *(describe)*:
9. ☐ The property claimed to be exempt consists of the loan value of unmatured life insurance policies (including endowment and annuity policies) or benefits from matured life insurance policies (including endowment and annuity policies). All other property of the same type owned by the judgment debtor or the spouse of the judgment debtor, either alone or in combination with others, is *(describe)*:

(14) → items 7, 8b, 9

I declare under penalty of perjury under the laws of the State of California that the foregoing is true and correct.

Date: (15)

(TYPE OR PRINT NAME) ▶ *(SIGNATURE OF CLAIMANT)*

Form Approved by the Judicial Council of California EJ-160 [New July 1, 1983]

CLAIM OF EXEMPTION
(Enforcement of Judgment)

CCP 703.520

INSTRUCTIONS FOR CLAIM OF EXEMPTION FORM

1. Put your name, mailing address and telephone number in this box. Put "in pro per" after "Attorney For."

2. Copy the name of the court as it is listed on the Notice of Levy served on you by the sheriff or marshal (e.g., Municipal Court for the Northern District of San Mateo County, 401 Redwood Dr., Redwood City, California).

3. The plaintiff's full name (the person who got the judgment against you) goes here.

4. Your full name goes here.

5. Put the Levying Officer's name and address here.

6. Put the Levying Officer's file number and the court case number here. These can be obtained from the Notice of Levy served on you by the sheriff or marshal.

7. Put your full name here (again).

8. Check this box.

9. Check this box unless you want notice of the court hearing to be sent to another address, in which case check the second box and put that address.

10. This box should be left blank unless the real judgment debtor is someone else. If so, put that person's last known address.

11. Here provide a brief description of the exempt property, e.g., "My 1973 Roadway Mobilehome (Serial No. 27423) in which I reside," or "My seasprite catamaran, docked at Slip #13, Alameda, CA., in which I reside"). If the property is described on the Notice of Levy, copy that description.

12. Here, put "C.C.P. Sections 704.20, 704.30, and 704.800."

13. Here, put the following statement: "I am entitled to a homestead exemption in the sum of $____________ (put your exemption amount here) out of the proceeds of the sale of said property, due to the property being the principal residence and dwelling of myself and _______________ (here put the name of your spouse or any person who makes up your family unit), now and at the time the judgment in this action was filed with the County Recorder."

NOTE: If you don't have room for this statement on the form, take a clean 8 1/2" by 11" piece of paper, label it "Attachment, Claim of Exemption, Number 6," and attach it to the main form.

14. Leave Boxes 7, 8, and 9 blank.

15. Date the form, print or type your name on the left, and sign on the right.

Make two photocopies, and deliver the original and one copy to the sheriff or marshal who served you WITHIN 10 DAYS OF THE DATE YOU WERE SERVED. Keep one copy for your own records.

After you have given these documents to the sheriff or marshal, the creditor will have 10 days to file an opposition to your claim of exemption with the sheriff or marshal. If this isn't done, your claim will succeed. If it is done, then the court hearing will occur. You may want to get an attorney to help you (see Appendix A), but you are probably safe enough representing yourself if your claim is straightforward. You must be prepared to establish:

1. The amount of exemption to which you are entitled; and

2. That you live in the living space in question and did so when the judgment was filed. The creditor may not even contest this point, but if he or she does, you should be ready to prove that it is your home. Some pictures of the inside of the living space would be helpful. Also, you can bring

some friends or neighbors who can testify on your behalf. Be sure the judge knows that your witnesses are present.

Assuming you are successful, the money you receive is exempt for six months from the date you receive it. If within six months you put the money into a new home in which you actually reside, the new home is automatically homesteaded. In addition, the exemption date on the new home harkens back to the date you started to reside in your old exempt home. This date is important since property is not exempt for purposes of judgment liens recorded before you or your spouse resided in your home.

<u>HAPPY NOTE</u>: Fortunately, in many cases your dwelling should be returned to you rather than sold, due to the

likelihood that the creditor would realize nothing from the sale. However, a malicious creditor may cause the sale to happen in the hopes that you don't reinvest your exempted amount within the six month period.

CHAPTER 12

Changing Status and Abandoning Your Homestead

A. Changing Your Status

As we've seen in earlier chapters, under Civil Code Section 704.730, the amount of your equity protected by a declared homestead probably depends on your status (single, head of household, disabled, etc.) at the time of the attempted sale of the homestead. This is a change from the former California law under which the amount of protected equity depended on your status at the time of filing. Does this mean that if your family status changes after you file, you now do not have to file a new Declaration of Homestead? Probably.

However, to be on the safe side, we recommend that you do file a new homestead declaration if your change in family status entitles you to a higher level of protection than when you initially filed. For example, if you file as a single individual and you are under 65 and not disabled, your protection is $30,000. If later you become disabled or have your 65th birthday, you may want to refile to be sure you qualify for protection at the $55,000 level. As we said, we believe you will qualify anyway, but because Civil Code Section 704.730 has yet to be interpreted by a court, and its wording is as muddy as the Sacramento River at flood stage, we feel it pays to be safe and refile.

If your status changes downward (i.e., you were part of a family unit when you filed a declaration for $45,000 but are now single, under 65, and not disabled), your original declaration is still valid, but your protection has probably decreased to $30,000.* Further, if the person who was originally part of your family unit subsequently moved out and filed a Declaration of Homestead, or claimed an automatic one, on another dwelling, your $45,000 protection would automatically drop to $30,000 due to the automatic abandonment provision (see Chapter 13). In this situation, there is no reason to refile.

What this all means is this:

- If you originally filed for $30,000, file for $45,000 or $55,000 if you become eligible (see Chapter 5).

---

* CALIFORNIA BANK V. SCHLESINGER (1958) 324 P.2d 119.

- If you originally filed for $45,000 or $55,000 but your situation has changed to the $30,000 category, you will probably be stuck with the lesser amount, but you need not refile.

IMPORTANT: Because the law is not at all clear on these points, we strongly recommend you consult an attorney if your home is being forcibly sold and the amount of your declared homestead exemption is an issue.

B. Abandoning Your Homestead

The law provides that a declared homestead may be abandoned either by declaration, or automatically when a new Declaration of Homestead is filed on other property.* In addition, selling the property also serves to abandon the homestead if it is sold by:

1. An unmarried person;

2. Both spouses;

* C.C.P. Sections 704.980, 990. See Chapter 7.

3. One spouse who was conveyed property by the other spouse and the latter failed to reserve any homestead rights in the deed;

4. A married person for his or her separate homestead.

NOTE: A conveyance of homesteaded property to your spouse does not in itself constitute an abandonment of the homestead. What happens in this situation is that the conveyance merely converts the property into the separate property of your spouse and the homestead continues in your spouse's favor.

Generally, you should never need to file an Abandonment of Declaration, since the law automatically considers your homestead abandoned when you file a new declaration on different property or when you sell the homesteaded property. In the event you do want to file a Declaration of Abandonment, however, we have provided the appropriate form and instructions in the back of the book. This will need to be filed in the same County Recorder's office where the Declaration of Homestead was recorded.

ADDITIONAL NOTE: Remember that if a new homestead declaration is filed by one person, it has no effect on any other person named in the prior homestead declaration unless they are also named in the new declaration. For example, if Tom and Jane, who have filed a homestead declaration on their home, break up, and Tom moves out and files a new homestead declaration on his new dwelling for himself only, Jane's interest is still protected ($30,000 or $45,000, depending on who else lives with Jane) but Tom's is automatically abandoned.

APPENDIX A

Choosing and Using A Lawyer (If You Decide You Need One)

Most people will find it easy to do their own homestead, but if you are the rare person with one of the few special problems noted in this book, then you may want to hire a lawyer. Finding a lawyer who charges reasonable prices and whom you feel can be trusted is not always an easy task. There is always the fear that by just picking a name out of the telephone book you may get someone unsympathetic or an attorney who will charge too much. Many people become a little intimidated when faced with selecting an attorney. Here are a few suggestions to ease the process:

1. Legal Aid: If you are very poor, you may qualify for free help from your Legal Aid Office. Check your phone directory for their location, or ask your County Clerk.

✓ 2. Group Legal Practices: A new but rapidly growing aspect of California law practice is the Group Legal Practice program. Many groups, including unions, employers and consumer action groups are offering plans to their members whereby they can get legal assistance for rates which are substantially lower than those offered by most private practitioners. Some of these plans are good, some mediocre, and a few are not worth it, but most are better than nothing. In the San Francisco Bay Area, a good plan is offered through the Consumer's Cooperative of Berkeley, Inc. Because the group practice area of the law is changing so rapidly, we can't give you a statewide list of group legal plans.

3. Private Attorneys: If you don't know an attorney who can be trusted and can't get a reliable recommendation from a friend, you have a problem. While you might be lucky and randomly pick an attorney who matches your needs perfectly, you might just as easily wind up paying too much for too little. Here are some suggestions that should make your search easier:

- Be wary of referral panels set up by local bar associations. Most lawyers can get on these panels by paying a fee. Membership on one of these panels normally demonstrates little or no special competence in the particular area of law for which

a referral is given. Many referral systems will charge you for the referral;

• Check with a local consumer organization to see if they can recommend someone;

• Shop around by calling different law offices and stating your problem. Ask them how much it would cost for a visit. Try to talk to a lawyer personally to attempt to get an idea of how friendly and sympathetic he is to your concerns;

• Remember, lawyers whose offices and life styles are reasonably simple are more likely to help you for less money than lawyers who feel naked unless wearing a $500 outfit. You should be able to find an attorney willing to discuss your problems for $50-$75;

• Recently lawyers have been permitted to advertise. Check the attorney section of your newspaper classified section.

APPENDIX B

Addresses of County Recorders

Mail or bring your form, along with $4.00, to the County Recorder at the address for your county, as listed below:

ALAMEDA
Room 105 Courthouse
1225 Fallon Street
Oakland, CA 94612

ALPINE
Box 266
Markleeville, CA 96120

AMADOR
108 Court Street
Jackson, CA 95642

BUTTE
Administration Building
25 County Center Drive
Oroville, CA 95965

CALAVERAS
Government Center
San Andreas, CA 95249

COLUSA
546 Jay Street
Colusa, CA 95932

CONTRA COSTA
Courthouse
725 Court St.
Martinez, CA 94553

DEL NORTE
Room 15 Courthouse
Crescent City, CA 95531

EL DORADO
360 Fair Lane
Placerville, CA 95667

FRESNO
Box 766
Fresno, CA 93721

GLENN
Courthouse
526 West Sycamore Street
Willows, CA 95988

HUMBOLDT
Courthouse
925 5th Street
Eureka, CA 95501

IMPERIAL
P.O. Box 1560
939 Main
El Centro, CA 92243

INYO
P.O. Drawer F
Independence, CA 93526

KERN
1415 Truxtun Av.
Bakersfield, CA 93301

KINGS
Gout Center
1400 W. Lacey Blvd.
Box 986
Hanford, CA 93230

LAKE
Courthouse
255 North Forbes Street
Lakeport, CA 95453

LASSEN
Courthouse
Susanville, CA 96130

LOS ANGELES
New Hall of Records, Rm. 5
227 North Broadway
Los Angeles, CA 90012

MADERA
209 W. Yosemite Av.
Madera, CA 93637

MARIN
Civic Center Hall of Justice
San Rafael, CA 94903

MARIPOSA
Box 156
Mariposa, CA 95338

MENDOCINO
Box 148
Room 103 Courthouse
Ukiah, CA 95482

MERCED
2222 M Street
Merced, CA 95340

MODOC
204 Court Street, Room 107
Alturas, CA 96101

MONO
Box 537
Courthouse
Bridgeport, CA 93517

MONTEREY
Courthouse, Box 1819
Salinas, CA 93902

NAPA
Hall of Records
1195 3rd Street
Napa, CA 94558

NEVADA
Courthouse
Nevada City, CA 95959

ORANGE
630 N. Broadway
Box 238
Santa Ana, CA 92702

PLACER
Dewitt Center
11546 B Avenue
Box 1547
Auburn, CA 95603

PLUMAS
Box 206
Quincy, CA 95971

RIVERSIDE
Box 751
Riverside, CA 92502

SACRAMENTO
901 G Street, Room 144
Sacramento, CA 95814

SAN BENITO
Room 206 Courthouse
Hollister, CA 95023

SAN BERNARDINO
172 W. 3rd St.
Second Floor
San Bernardino, CA 92415

SAN DIEGO
1600 Pacific Hwy
Room 260
San Diego, CA 92101

SAN FRANCISCO
Room 167 City Hall
San Francisco, CA 94102

SAN JOAQUIN
24 S. Hunter, Rm. 304
Stockton, CA 95201

SAN LUIS OBISPO
Courthouse 102
San Luis Obispo, CA 93408

SAN MATEO
Hall of Justice & Records
Redwood City, CA 94063

SANTA BARBARA
P.O. Drawer CC
Santa Barbara, CA 93102

SANTA CLARA
70 W. Hedding St.
San Jose, CA 95113

SANTA CRUZ
701 Ocean Street
Room 110
Santa Cruz, CA 95060

SHASTA
Courthouse, Room 105
Redding, CA 96001

SIERRA
Drawer D
Downieville, CA 95936

SISKIYOU
Box 8
Yreka, CA 96097

SOLANO
Courthouse
Fairfield, CA 94533

SONOMA
585 Fiscal Drive
Box 6124
Santa Rosa, CA 95406

STANISLAUS
800 11th St., Rm. 123
Modesto, CA 95354

SUTTER
463 2nd Street
Yuba City, CA 95991

TEHAMA
Courthouse
Box 250
Red Bluff, CA 96080

TRINITY
Box AK
Weaverville, CA 96093

TULARE
203 County Civic Center
Visalia, CA 93277

TUOLOMNE
2 So. Green Street
Sonora, CA 95370

VENTURA
800 S. Victoria Avenue
Ventura, CA 93009

YOLO
725 Court Street, Rm. 200
Woodland, CA 95695

YUBA
Courthouse
215 Fifth Street
Marysville, CA 95901

APPENDIX C

Officials to Write to Demand Increased Homestead Protections

The homestead law exists because the Constitution of the State of California says it must. It exists to protect you. The writers of the Constitution wanted Californians to have protection from the forced sale of their homes even though they got behind on their bills. The State Legislature has interpreted the constitutional requirement in a way that limits the protection to either $30,000, $45,000 or $55,000.*

These figures are not permanent ones, as from time to time the Legislature will adjust them upwards to keep them in line with the current economy.

Ideally, the homestead protection should be an automatic one. The filing

---

* This is expected to increase to $60,000, effective January 1, 1987. Proposed increases for families and non-elderly or disabled individuals failed to survive the legislative process.

of a homestead declaration should not be required, and everyone who owns or is buying a home should be protected. Certainly it is not fair that people can end up with reduced protection just because they did not know how to get a homestead on file.

One suspects that the current situation is the result of lobbying and interference by mercenary interests. Therefore, it is important to do some lobbying on your own to promote your own interests.

A letter to your state legislators or other elected state officials expressing your opinion that the homestead protection should be automatic, and/or the protection amounts increased, may result in focusing the attention of California legislators on expanding homestead protections. The government has not succeeded in protecting the value of your income, but the least it could do would be to increase the protection of your home.

Here is an example of a letter you can send to your state representatives:

1500 Acorn St., #4
Cloverdale, Calif.
June 1, 1986

Dear Senator or Assemblyperson________________:

I believe that legislation should be passed to extend homestead protections to anyone who owns or is buying a home automatically. The present so-called automatic homestead law is not adequate to do this as it has been interpreted to provide less protection than the declared homestead law. All Californians should have the security of not having their homes sold from under them as was the original intention of the homestead provision of the California State Constitution.

Legislation should also be introduced to raise the amounts protected. As our money becomes worth less and less, existing protection amounts become more and more inadequate. I feel that a family should be entitled to a good, solid home, free of the threat of a forced sale. This means that equity in a home should be protected to at least the $100,000 level.

Many Californians would benefit from any action taken in these directions. Thank you for your consideration of this letter.

Sincerely,

Trudy Ahlstrom

Forms and Instructions

This is where you sit down, relax, and take a look at the instructions on how to do it. It's really easy--the fact that there are even as many words as you see here is mainly due to our desire to be perfectly clear. All that you actually do is 1) fill in your name(s); 2) choose the appropriate filing category; 3) add the legal description of your property; 4) check whether the home is your principal dwelling or that of your spouse; 5) notarize it; and 6) file it. On the next page, we show you an illustration of the "Declaration of Homestead" form found at the rear of the book. The circled numbers refer to the instructions that follow the form, referred to as "items." By the time you actually fill in the tear-out form at the end of the book, you should have a clear idea of what you're doing.

DECLARATION OF HOMESTEAD

1 1. ☐ I ______________________________

☐ We ______________________________

and ______________________________

do hereby declare:

2 2. a. ☐ We are husband and wife

b. ☐ I am a member of a family unit consisting of myself and ____________________

______________________________.

c. ☐ My birthdate is ______________ ☐ My spouse's birthdate is ______________

d. ☐ I am disabled ☐ My spouse is disabled

e. ☐ I am an individual.

3 3. ☐ I ☐ We now reside on that land and premises in the City of ________________,

County of ______________________, State of California, known and described as follows:

4 4. This is the principal dwelling of ☐ the declared homestead owner or ☐ the declared homestead owner's spouse.

5 5. ☐ I ☐ We hereby claim and declare said premises as a homestead for ☐ my benefit ☐ our joint benefit.

6. The facts stated in this Declaration are true as of my/our personal knowledge.

DATED: ______________________

____
DECLARANT

____
DECLARANT

STATE OF CALIFORNIA
COUNTY OF ______________________ } SS

On ______________________________, 19__,
before me, the undersigned, a Notary Public in and for said State, personally appeared
______________________________,
personally known to me (or proved to me on the basis of satisfactory evidence) to be the person(s) whose name(s) is/are subscribed to the within instrument, and severally acknowledged to me that (s)he/they executed the same.

Witness my hand and official seal.

____
Notary Public in and for said State

FILLING OUT THE FORM

Item #1

You should either check the first box and put your name in the blank if you are the only person declaring the homestead, or check the second box and put both your name and your spouse's name in the following space if you are married and declaring the homestead jointly. If you are married but the house is owned as your separate property, check the first box.

NOTE: Make sure that your name here is the same as your signature. For example, if in Item #1 you use the name "JOHN MILTON DOE," sign your name the same way, not "JOHN M. DOE," or "J.M. DOE." County recorders are notoriously particular when it comes to names being exactly the same throughout.

Item #2

Check the box on line a if you are declaring as husband and wife.

Check the box on line b if you are declaring as part of a family unit, and put the name of the person who qualifies you to declare as a family unit. If you are married but own the house as your separate property, check the second box and put the name of your spouse or other individual as the person who qualifies you as a household unit. See Chapter 5 for details on who this might be.

Fill in the appropriate birthdates on line c. If you are already 65, or later turn 65 while this declaration is on file, your birthdate will provide notice of this fact. See Chapter 5.

Check the appropriate box on line d if you or your spouse is disabled. See Chapter 5 for the meaning of disabled.

Check the box on line e if you are declaring as an individual, are under 65, and not disabled.

NOTE: If you check the boxes on line a or b, your exemption will be $45,000. If you check any of the boxes on lines c or d, your exemption is $55,000. If you check the box on line e, your exemption is $30,000.

Item #3

This part of your form contains the location and legal description of your property. In the blanks provided, you type in the name of the city and county where your place is located. If you are not within any city limits, then just leave that part blank and enter the name of the county. Following the words "known and described as follows:" you must type in the legal description found on your deed. It will be found near the center of the deed following the phrase "known and described as follows:" The legal description may consist merely of a reference to a lot number on a certain map on file with the County Recorder, or it may go into metes and bounds as well. Either way, include on your homestead everything from your deed which appears to describe your property. If you have trouble finding the deed, you can get a copy of it from the County Recorder. If you are not certain which part of it is the legal description, ask any friendly realtor or title company. Some deeds have extremely lengthy descriptions. An elaborate description may take up more space than we have provided on the form. If this is the case, don't abbreviate the description but continue it on a second sheet of paper which can then be attached by stapling it to the first form. An additional $1.00 fee will be charged for filing a second sheet.

Item #4:

If the judgment debtor uses the home as his or her principal residence, check the first box. If the judgment debtor has moved, but the spouse remains, check the second box.

Item #5:

Check the apppropriate box, depending on whether you are an individual or joint declarant. Then date and sign the same name as appears in item #1.

NOTARIZATION

Once you have filled out the form, it must be sworn to and signed in the presence of a Notary Public. If it is a joint declaration by husband and wife, then both must appear and sign before the Notary. You will be asked to produce identification unless the Notary already knows who you are. Notaries can be found at most real estate offices, county offices, law offices, banks and in many libraries. If you have a problem locating one, check the Yellow Pages.

FILING

After notarization and signing, the homestead declaration can either be mailed in or taken personally to the County Recorder for the county in which your property is located. Appendix B contains a list of all California county recorders and their addresses. The declaration must be accompanied by a money order for $4.ØØ. Include a self-addressed, stamped envelope because when they finish recording the document, it will be returned to you. Meanwhile, it's a good idea if you have a photocopy made of it before you submit it, just in case it gets lost.

INSTRUCTIONS FOR ABANDONMENT

The second form in the back of this book is for use in case you wish to file a Declaration of Abandonment of Homestead.

The illustration on the next page shows the abandonment form and how it is filled in. This is followed by notes giving details on each item of the form.

DECLARATION OF ABANDONMENT OF HOMESTEAD

(1) 1. I, (we) ____,

do hereby declare:

(2) 2. I (we) hereby abandon the homestead heretofore declared by me (us) on ______________,

19___, on those premises known and described as follows:

(2) the declaration of which homestead was recorded on ____________________, 19___, in

Book ________, Page ________, of the ____________________ records of

________________________ County, California.

____
DECLARANT

DATED: ________________________

____
DECLARANT

STATE OF CALIFORNIA
COUNTY OF ____________________ } SS

On ____, 19___,
before me, the undersigned, a Notary Public in and for said State, personally appeared
____,
personally known to me (or proved to me on the basis of satisfactory evidence) to be the person(s) whose name(s) is/are subscribed to the within instrument, and severally acknowledged to me that (s)he/they executed the same.

Witness my hand and official seal.

____
Notary Public in and for said State

FILLING OUT THE FORM

Item #1

This is simply the name(s) of the person(s) making the declaration. There is room for two names so that a husband and wife who previously joined in a homestead may now join in its abandonment. An individual may also use this same form. Be consistent in the use of your name. Use exactly the same form of your name as appears on the previous homestead agreement, and stick to that form throughout. For example: the name "JOHN MILTON DOE" should not later appear as "JOHN M. DOE."

Item #2

This requires the date the former homestead declaration was filed, followed by the exact legal description as it appeared on that document. This information can be gotten from a copy of the former declaration. If you have lost your copy, you can obtain a new one from the County Recorder for the county in which the declaration was filed.

The first blanks of Item #2 are filled in with the date on which the former declaration was signed. This is followed by the legal description of the property, exactly as it appears on the former document. The last blanks are for the recording information, which can usually be found on the original document, stamped onto the upper or lower margin of the document. This shows the date of recordation and the Book and

Page numbers of the County Records into which it was entered.

NOTARIZATION

The document is now dated, signed and notarized. If two people sign the document, both signatures must be notarized. You can find a Notary in most real estate or insurance offices, banks or libraries.

FILING

Mail or hand deliver the notarized Abandonment to the County Recorder of the county in which the original Declaration of Homestead was filed, along with a money order for $4.00 to cover the filing fee. Send a self-addressed, stamped envelope for the return of the document. Save it for your files once it is returned to you. A Declaration of Abandonment becomes effective only from the time it is recorded.

How To Form Your Own California Corporation
All the forms, Bylaws, Articles, stock certificates and instructions necessary to file your small profit corporation in California.
California Edition $24.95
Texas Edition $21.95
New York Edition $19.95

The Non-Profit Corporation Handbook
Includes all the forms, Bylaws, Articles and instructions you need to form a non-profit corporation in California.
California Only $24.95

Bankruptcy: Do It Yourself
Step-by-step instructions and all the forms you need.
National Edition $14.95

Legal Care For Your Software
Protect your software through the use of trade secret, trademark, copyright, patents, contracts and agreements.
National Edition $24.95

The Dictionary of Intellectual Property Law
Provides functional and contextual definitions for the hundreds of law-related terms commonly used in high technology computer commerce.
National Edition $17.95

The Partnership Book
A basic primer for people who are starting a small business together. Sample agreements, buy-out clauses, limited partnerships.
National Edition $17.95

Plan Your Estate: Wills, Probate Avoidance, Trusts and Taxes
Making a will, alternatives to probate, living trusts, limiting inheritance and estate taxes, and more.
California Edition $15.95
Texas Edition $14.95

WillWriter - a software/book package
Use your computer to prepare and update your own valid will. Runs on Apple II+, IIe, IIc, the Mac, the IBM PC (and most PC compatibles).
National Edition $49.95

Nolo's Simple Will Book
Shows you how to draft a will without a lawyer in any state except Louisiana.
National Edition $12.95

The Power of Attorney Book
Covers the process which allows you to arrange for someone else to protect your rights and property should you become incapable of doing so.
National Edition $14.95

Chapter 13: The Federal Plan to Repay Your Debts
The alternative to straight bankruptcy. This book helps you develop a plan to pay your debts over a three year period. All forms and worksheets included.
National Edition $12.95

Billpayers' Rights
Bankruptcy, student loans, bill collectors and collection agencies, credit cards, car repossessions, child support, etc.
California only $12.95

The California Professional Corporation Handbook
All the forms and instructions to form a professional corporation.
California only $24.95

Small Time Operator
How to start and operate your own small business, keep books and pay taxes.
National Edition $9.95

How to Settle a Simple Estate
Forms and instructions necessary to wind up a California resident's estate after death.
California Edition $19.95

How to Do Your Own Divorce
All the forms for an uncontested dissolution. Instructions included.
California Edition $12.95
Texas Edition $12.95

California Marriage and Divorce Law
Community and separate property, debts, children, buying a house, etc. Sample pre-nuptial contracts, simple will, probate avoidance information.
California only $14.95

The Child Support Handbook
How to change and enforce child support payments. Complete with forms and instructions.
California only $14.95

The Living Together Kit
Legal guide for unmarried couples. Covers wills, living together contracts, children, medical emergencies, etc.
National Edition $14.95

Sourcebook For Older Americans
Most comprehensive resource tool on income, rights and benefits of Americans over 55. Social security, Medicare, pensions, etc.
National Edition $12.95

How to Adopt Your Stepchild
How to prepare all forms and appear in court.
California only $17.95

A Legal Guide for Lesbian/Gay Couples
Raising children, buying property, wills, job discrimination and more.
National Edition $17.95

Start Up Money: How to Finance Your New Small Business
How to write a business plan, obtain a loan package and find sources of finance.
National Edition $12.95

Patent It Yourself
Complete instructions on how to do a patent search and file a patent in the U.S.
National Edition $24.95

How to Copyright Software
Covers common mistakes and how to correct them, failure to register, problems with protection and the Computer Copyright Act.
National Edition $21.95

The People's Law Review
50-state catalog of self-help law materials, articles and interviews.
National Edition $8.95

Fight Your Ticket
Preparing for court, arguing your case, cross-examining witnesses, etc.
California only $12.95

Legal Research: How to Find and Understand the Law
Comprehensive guide to doing your own legal research.
National Edition $14.95

Tenants' Rights
Everything tenants need to know to protect themselves.
California Edition $14.95
Texas Edition $6.95

Everybody's Guide to Small Claims Court
Step-by-step guide to going to small claims court and collecting a judgment.
California Edition $10.95
National Edition $10.95